Inventions That Shaped the World

THE COTTON GIN

NANCY ROBINSON MASTERS

Franklin Watts
A Division of Scholastic Inc.
New York • Toronto • London • Auckland • Sydney
Mexico City • New Delhi • Hong Kong
Danbury, Connecticut

Photographs © 2006: Art Resource, NY: 16 (Charles Le Brun/Reunion des Musees Nationaux), 14 (Erich Lessing); Bridgeman Art Library International Ltd., London/New York: 11 (Brooklyn Museum of Art, New York, USA, John Thomas Underwood Memorial Fund), 36 (Dallas Historical Society, Texas, USA); Corbis Images: cover bottom left, cover bottom right, 28, 29, 43 (Bettmann), cover background, chapter opener, 70, 71 (Richard T. Nowitz), 66 (Jim Sugar), cover top left (Underwood & Underwood), 65, 68 (Michael S. Yamashita), 54; Culver Pictures: 17, 19, 20, 24, 47; Georgia Historical Society, Savannah, Georgia: 25, 26; Getty Images: 52 (Collection Roger-Viollet), 22 (Stock Montage/Hulton Archive), 45 (Medford Taylor/National Geographic); Library of Congress: 32; National Cotton Council: 9, 62; North Wind Picture Archives: 40; Samford University Library, Birmingham, Alabama: 57; Superstock, Inc./Jose Perovani: 42; Telfair Museum of Art: 6; U.S. Postal Service: 5; USDA Cotton Ginning Research Unit: 44.

Illustrations by J. T. Morrow

Cover design by The Design Lab
Book production by The Design Lab

Library of Congress Cataloging-in-Publication Data
Robinson Masters, Nancy.
  The cotton gin / Nancy Robinson Masters.
  p. cm. — (Inventions that shaped the world)
  Includes bibliographical references and index.
  ISBN 0-531-12406-1 (lib. bdg.)   0-531-13901-8 (pbk.)
  1. Inventors—United States—Biography—Juvenile literature. 1. Whitney, Eli, 1765–1825. 2. Inventors.] I. Title. II. Series.
  TS1570.W4R63 2005
  677'.2121—dc22   2005008051

CONTENTS

The Picture on the Stamp

"Eli Whitney and the cotton gin fostered the invention spirit in all of us."
—Induction remarks, National Inventors Hall of Fame, 1974

The Eli Whitney one-cent stamp was one of five stamps issued by the United States Postal Service in 1940 to honor great inventors.

A one-cent postage stamp issued by the United States Post Office in 1940 bears the portrait of Eli Whitney. The stamp honors Whitney as one of five great inventors in a series of "Famous Americans" stamps issued that year.

Although many individuals played a variety of roles in the history, invention, and development of the cotton *gin,* Whitney is the person most often identified with

Catherine Greene was the widow of Revolutionary War general Nathanael Greene and owned Mulberry Grove Plantation near Savannah, Georgia.

perfecting a machine for separating lint from cottonseed. He and his partner, Phineas Miller, were the right men in the right place at the right time who helped to bring about a change in mechanical separation of cotton fibers from seeds that continues to impact the world today.

The Industrial Revolution, a period that began in England in the eighteenth century when machinery was rapidly replacing manual labor to produce goods, was under way when Whitney was born in 1765. He arrived at Mulberry Grove—a rice plantation located on a bluff above Georgia's Savannah River—in 1793 as a recent graduate of Yale College. He was a guest of Miller and plantation owner Catherine Greene, to whom Miller was engaged. The United States was still recovering from its struggles to win the Revolutionary War and to become economically independent.

The British who settled at Jamestown in the early 1600s brought cottonseed to America to determine if the crop would grow in the colony. Colonists were forbidden to manufacture cotton goods, but grew cotton for export to England and for their own personal use. In turn, they purchased cotton goods from Great Britain. **Textile** imports from Great Britain were stopped during the war, so colonists began planting more cotton to supply their needs. By the time Whitney arrived at Mulberry Grove, the Industrial Revolution was beginning to spread through Europe. Cotton, cotton, and more cotton was needed to keep the machines spinning and weaving thread.

Miller, Greene, and other planters knew planting more cotton and less rice would not be profitable unless some method could be found to separate the seeds from the cotton more quickly. Roller gins, which squeezed the black seeds from long-**staple** Sea Island cotton (*staple* refers to fiber length), had been used for hundreds of years. But these gins did not work well with short-staple upland cotton, which contained tiny green seeds. While upland cotton grew far better in most locations than Sea Island cotton, one person picking out the tiny green seeds by hand could produce only about 1 pound (0.5 kilogram) of lint a day.

The Long and Short of It

Staple refers to the length of the cotton fibers after the seeds and trash have been removed. Short-staple cotton fibers are less than 25 millimeters (not quite 1 inch) in length. Long-staple cotton fibers are 30 millimeters or longer. Fibers between 25 and 30 millimeters are considered medium staple. Fibers 37 millimeters or longer are designated as extra-long staple, also known as Pima cotton.

The small difference between the staple lengths makes a huge difference in how cotton is made into thread, woven into cloth, and sold.

After hearing Whitney's ideas for a cotton gin to use for upland cotton, Miller eagerly agreed to finance his invention efforts. Miller, as much as Whitney, hoped to achieve fame and fortune for his efforts, although Miller may have wondered what the world was going to do with all the cotton that would be ginned if Whitney's idea proved successful.

CHAPTER TWO

Why Cotton?

Porque Algodao? Perche Cotone? Pourquio Coton? Porque Algodon?
"Why Cotton?" in Portuguese, Italian, French, and Spanish

If Phineas Miller had stepped out of Eli Whitney's work shed in 1793 and into one of today's huge shopping malls, he would immediately be surrounded by what the world has done with so much cotton. Clothes, rugs, sheets, shoes, towels, and upholsteries are the most recognizable items made of cotton.

Many of the products you use everyday, such as bath towels, are made of cotton.

9

Not as easily recognizable as cotton products are books, camera film, cosmetics, medical supplies, sports equipment, toothpaste, and even paper money. Cotton fiber makes up 75 percent of all new paper currency in the United States.

Cotton Conquers Counterfeits

Genuine United States currency paper has tiny red and blue cotton fibers embedded throughout. Counterfeiters try to imitate these fibers by printing tiny red and blue lines on their paper. Close inspection reveals that on the counterfeit bill, the lines are printed on the surface, not embedded in the paper.

Spreading the Seeds of Survival

Plants and animals provided the raw material for the first textiles. Archaeologists have found evidence that woven grasses and vines were used to hold skins and fur together for crude clothing worn by prehistoric people. Leaves and bark tied by vines to feet were the first shoes.

Agronomists are scientists who study crops. They believe the first cotton plants grew in Africa, Asia, and South America. As populations increased in those areas, people had to travel greater distances to find adequate food and water. Nomadic groups carrying baskets and mats woven with cotton fibers scattered the seeds.

While studying some of the earliest civilizations, agronomists and archaeologists made an amazing discovery: They found bits of woven cotton cloth more than six thousand years old in ancient caves in Mexico. This cloth would have been made at about the same time that the first silk material was being produced in China—making cotton one of the oldest known textiles.

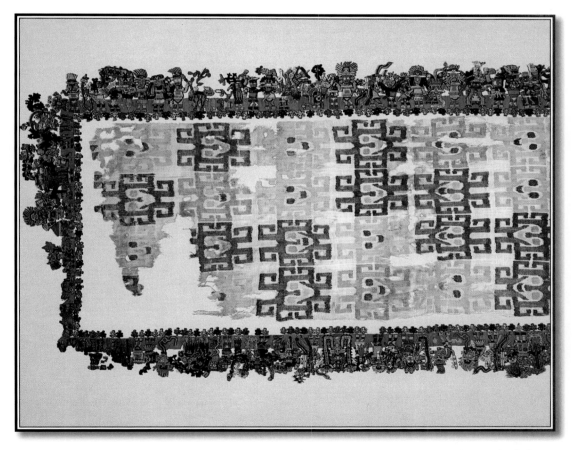

People have been weaving cotton into cloth for thousands of years. These cloth fragments made of cotton and wool were made in Peru in the first century.

White Gold

By 1000 B.C., people in India were planting and harvesting cotton to make into cloth. Cotton pulled through a churka (sometimes spelled charkha) roller gin could be spun on a **spinning wheel** into threads so fine that 1 pound (0.5 kg) of fiber produced 73 yards (67 meters) of material!

The popularity of Indian cotton is still evidenced by the number of words for cotton fabrics that have made their way into the English language: *calico*, *gingham*, *chintz*, and *khaki* are well-known words of Indian origin in our fabric vocabulary.

Making Cloth from Cotton

Cotton is a member of the mallow plant family. The shrubby plants produce white blooms followed by small green seedpods called *bolls.* Fibers grow inside the bolls.

Cloth is made from cotton in five steps:

1. Cottonseeds are planted in loose soil in mild to hot climates.
2. The cotton is harvested when it produces fibers.
3. The seeds are separated from the fiber.
4. The fibers are spun into threads.
5. The threads are woven into cloth.

The Churka Roller Gin and the Spinning Wheel

Eli Whitney did not invent the first machine used to separate cottonseeds from cotton fiber. A machine called the churka roller gin was in use at least three thousand years ago in India. It is called a gin, which is short for engine, even though it relied completely on human power.

The churka roller gin removed the seeds from cotton by pinching and pulling the seeds out of the lint as the fiber passed through a set of rollers. This method worked fairly well on long-staple cotton because the seeds in long-staple cotton are not sticky like those in short-staple cotton.

The spinning wheel was probably invented in India about the same time as the churka roller gin, though no one knows for sure who invented either of these machines. The spinning wheel turned fibers into thread, which were then woven into cloth on a *loom.*

Mysterious and Sacred

Garments made of finely woven cotton were considered sacred in some ancient cultures. In Egypt, for example, only the high priest was allowed to wear a cotton garment.

African cultures such as the Ashanti people of Ghana and the Sakalava and Mahafaly people of Madagascar believed the act of cleaning, spinning, and weaving cotton fibers gave magical powers to cotton cloth. They made offerings to their looms, believing supernatural spirits actually lived in the threads.

Chensumose, the priest of Amun-Ra, appears in this illustration from the ancient Egyptian Book of the Dead. In ancient Egypt, only high priests were allowed to wear cotton garments.

Cotton thread was also thought to have the power to cure diseases. Several cultures believed that a charm made of cotton thread wrapped around a tooth, piece of bone, or lock of hair ensured the wearer would recover from an illness.

The Spider Ananse

Ananse, the weaver spider, began as a fictitious character in African folklore symbolizing the strengths and weaknesses of the African people. Artisans in Ghana were famous for making exquisite fabric known as kente cloth. As they wove the prized cloth in white and different colors, entire villages gathered to listen to these weavers tell stories about Ananse's wisdom and trickery.

The spider continues today as the unifying symbol of all African peoples. Ananse tales have become popular as written stories. (Written versions sometimes use the spelling Anansi.)

Common Cloth

Cotton was first brought into Europe from India in about 300 B.C., during the time of Alexander the Great. The Arabic peoples called it *qutun*, which is where the word *cotton* comes from.

When Christopher Columbus arrived in North America in 1492, can you guess what he found growing in the Bahamas islands? He found cotton plants producing

Alexander the Great was born in 356 B.C. and died in 323 B.C.

16

A slave on a cotton plantation was required to pick 150 to 200 pounds (68 to 91 kg) of cotton each day.

long-staple cotton firmly rooted in the New World. Among the gifts he received from the native Arawak people were balls of cotton thread grown on the island of San Salvador.

Old Ways in the New World

Slavery, the practice of keeping human beings as property, did not begin in the American colonies. It has been part of numerous cultures since the beginning of recorded history, and is still practiced in some cultures today.

In 1793, each state in the United States determined whether it would allow slavery, even though many citizens were personally opposed to slavery. Before the northern states banned slavery, slaves there primarily worked on ships, in factories, and in mills.

In the southern states where agriculture was the primary industry, slaves mostly planted, tended, and harvested crops. Planters paid as much as $300 for a healthy young field slave. By 1791, one-third of Georgia's population were slaves.

A Day in the Life of Solomon Northrup

Solomon Northrup was kidnapped in New York and sold as a slave in Louisiana. His description of a day working on a cotton plantation is part of an oral interview in the National Archives of the United States:

"The hands [slaves] are required to be in the cotton field by daylight. With the exception of fifteen minutes which is given to them at noon to eat an allowance of cold bacon, they are not permitted a moment idle until it is too dark to see.

"The day's work over in the field, the cotton must be carried to the gin house to be weighed. If it falls short in the weight he is appointed to have, he must suffer. And if he has exceeded what is expected, his master will wonder why he has not done this much in the past. So, whether he has too little or too much, the approach to the gin house is always with fear."

Most small planters in the southern states did not own slaves. They and their families did all of the work required to produce a cotton crop that often did not provide enough

Workers make cloth in a factory in England in 1776.

money for their basic needs. These planters needed the cotton gin to make their farms profitable as much as the larger plantation owners did.

The Age of Invention

While the American colonies were busy establishing their independence, Great Britain was experiencing the Industrial Revolution. The Industrial Revolution was a period of economic and social change that began in England in about 1730, when England's agricultural society began to move toward becoming a more urban, industrial society. With the invention of the steam engine in 1769, factory workers began to outnumber farm laborers in England. More textile factories needed more cotton!

English inventors set the stage for the revolution in textile manufacturing. An American named Eli Whitney would play the starring role in the invention of a better cotton gin.

Inventions That Created the Demand for More Cotton

- The Spinning Jenny—In 1764, James Hargreaves improved an earlier invention by Thomas Highs

  This hand-powered spinning wheel (below) made it possible for a spinner to produce more than one thread at a time.

- The Water Frame—Actual inventor is unknown, though it was put into use in about 1769

  This water-powered spinning machine was used to spin cotton thread.

- The Spinning Mule—Invented by Samuel Crompton in 1779

  This machine made it possible for one person to operate up to one thousand spindles at a time, which drew out cotton fiber and twisted it together to produce thread.

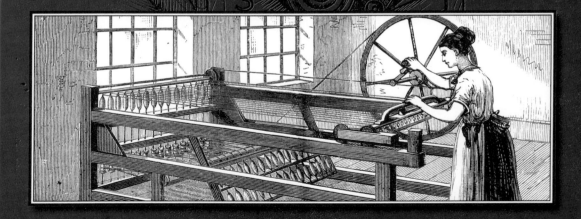

CHAPTER THREE

Man of Myth and Marvels

"I had better pursue it."—Eli Whitney, in a letter to his father, September 11, 1793

Eli Whitney's life was a mixture of myths and marvels. Most of the myths are the result of an article that first appeared in the 1832 edition of *The American Journal of Science*, and was later published in 1846 as the book, *Memoir of Eli Whitney, Esq.* (Some recent researchers believe author Denison Olmsted, a respected professor of natural philosophy and astronomy at Yale College, wrote a flattering, but not completely factual, biography of Whitney. Olmsted relied heavily upon information provided by Whitney's sister, Betsy, to describe Whitney's early childhood.)

Whitney was born December 8, 1765, in Westborough, Massachusetts. He spent his childhood like other boys in the decade before the American Revolution learning to "read, figure and measure." These were subjects every

Eli Whitney was born in 1765. This portrait was made when he was about fifty years old.

middle-class boy was expected to study, according to Dale Taylor, author of *Everyday Life in Colonial America*.

By the time the United States declared its independence from British rule in 1776, Whitney's interest in making things with his hands far outweighed his interest in scholarly pursuits. According to Olmsted, he preferred taking apart his father's watch and then reassembling it to reading the classics of literature. Neighbors considered Eli a shy boy who enjoyed building a violin of his own design more than attending parties or socials. He turned to these natural mechanical skills to work through the grief he experienced at the age of twelve when his mother died.

Maker of Nails and Hatpins

Much to the surprise of his father and stepmother, fourteen-year-old Eli began to talk of attending Yale College to study "useful arts." He built his own **forge** and made or repaired tools such as hoes, axes, and plows as a blacksmith. He knew he would have to earn the money to pay for college.

Not content to do the ordinary, young Whitney invented a nail-making machine. With adequate supplies of iron, the teenage entrepreneur made more than three thousand nails a day! Success as a nail maker inspired him to make hatpins. Ladies used hatpins to secure their hats to their hair. For a time, he was the only manufacturer of ladies' hatpins in the country, according to Olmsted's memoir.

From Dream to Degree

Whitney's father and stepmother initially discouraged him from attending Yale College. His father, however, eventually lent him some money to help pay some of his fees. At age twenty-one, Whitney took the school's entrance test—and passed.

In spite of his father's help, Whitney did not have enough money saved to pay his tuition. He took a job as a teacher in a private school in a nearby town, saving every penny of his salary to pay for college. The determined Whitney finally entered Yale when he was twenty-three years old. He graduated at the top of his class four years later. He was fluent in Greek and Latin and had a reputation as a superb mechanic, but he also had debts he could not pay and little hope of finding a job that suited him.

Yale College

Yale College was founded in 1701 as the Collegiate School in the home of Abraham Pierson in Killingworth, Connecticut. In 1716, the school moved to New Haven. Two years later, the school was renamed for Elihu Yale, who had supplied the college with a large gift that included books and goods. It became Yale University in 1887.

At the time Eli Whitney applied to attend, all students at Yale were male and most were studying for careers in the ministry or law. Today, Yale is a large research university with more than eleven thousand men and women enrolled as students in a wide assortment of programs.

Mulberry Grove was a rice plantation that belonged to Nathanael Greene and his wife Catherine. When he died, Catherine ran the plantation with the help of plantation manager Phineas Miller who she later married.

Turning Point

The president of Yale told Whitney about a teaching position in South Carolina that he should apply for. He booked passage on a sailing vessel out of New York that was also carrying Phineas Miller, an earlier Yale graduate. Miller introduced Whitney to Catherine Greene, a widow whose plantation, Mulberry Grove, Miller managed and to whom he was engaged. (Mrs. Greene was the widow of Revolutionary War hero Nathanael Greene.)

Whitney later wrote in a letter to his father that after the ship arrived in Savannah, Georgia, he traveled the 12 miles (19 kilometers) to Mulberry Grove Plantation with

Mulberry Grove was located near Savannah, Georgia. Catherine Greene sold the plantation in 1800. The house and other buildings were burned by General Sherman's troops in 1864 during the American Civil War.

Mrs. Greene and Miller, expecting to spend four or five days there before traveling to South Carolina to assume the teaching job.

"During this time I heard much said of the extreme difficulty of ginning cotton, that is, separating it from its seeds. There were a number of very respectable gentlemen at Mrs. Greene's who all agreed that if a machine could be invented which would clean the cotton with expedition, it would be a great thing both to the Country and to the inventor."

Whitney told his father he had "involuntarily happened to be thinking on the subject and struck out a plan of a machine in my mind." (His ideas for inventions often came while he was "involuntarily thinking.")

When Whitney told Miller about his plan, Miller urged him to pursue it, offering to finance the cost—with the understanding they would share the profits if it succeeded.

Whitney's fate seemed to be sealed when he arrived at the teaching job and was informed that the salary would be only half the amount that had been agreed upon. He rejected the position and returned to Mulberry Grove. There, he partnered with Miller to invent a machine that, unlike earlier machines, would rapidly separate cotton fiber from the seeds. The decision to return to the plantation would be one of the most important turning points in Whitney's life.

Mulberry Grove Plantation Today

Moss-covered piles of bricks are all that remain of the plantation home at Mulberry Grove where Eli Whitney lived while inventing his cotton gin. Only low mounds of the round chimney stones of the original sheds and slave quarters are visible.

The Georgia Port Authority owns the 2,200-acre (890-hectare) plantation. Some groups want to reconstruct the buildings and open Mulberry Grove as a historic site. The U.S. Fish and Wildlife Service wants to acquire the property and add it to the Savannah National Wildlife Refuge. For now, the only occupants of Mulberry Grove are birds and wildlife.

From Success to Sorrow

Whitney worked for ten days to make a cotton gin model that could do what roller-type gins could not do. It took another seven months to make a full-size working cotton gin. He was able to keep his invention "a profound secret" until he agreed to show it to some of Mrs. Greene's planter friends.

A painting of Eli Whitney in the shed where he worked on his cotton gin

Whitney's original cotton gin is in the National Museum of American History.

Whitney and Miller formed their partnership on May 27, 1793. They agreed Whitney would return to New Haven to secure a **patent** and open a factory to build gins. Whitney and Miller originally planned to own all of the gins and clean cotton for the planters. Rather than sell the gins, they would collect 1 pound (0.5 kg) of clean cotton for every 3 pounds (1.4 kg) they ginned. This toll, or charge, would result in a **monopoly** that would make them extremely wealthy. They would control all the ginning by owning all the gins. What the partners failed to consider was the ability of the planters to have mechanics construct their own gins after seeing Whitney's simple design.

In 1795, fire destroyed the New Haven factory when some workers left it unoccupied while they went out for a meal. The cause of the fire was unknown. "All my tools, material and work equal to twenty finished cotton machines all gone," Whitney wrote his father.

This disaster was followed by years of lawsuits the partners pursued trying to claim the earnings from their patent rights. As Miller had predicted, the South became a sea of white cotton. Gins whirred on every plantation, but the sound was not music to Whitney's ears because most of the gins did not belong to him and Miller. Planters unwilling to pay the toll to the partners had arranged for construction of their own gins. During the next ten years, the partners battled through an estimated sixty lawsuits, arguing their claims to the patent rights. Although they eventually won most of the lawsuits, the money they received did not repay them for the time lost and expenses incurred.

From Sorrow to Success

Eli Whitney's career as an inventor could have ended with the cotton gin, but it did not. He returned to New Haven to pursue producing muskets for the U.S. Army. Here again, myth and fact collide. Whitney has often been credited with inventing the method of manufacturing that uses **interchangeable parts.** Scholars now believe these claims are based upon legend more than fact because the concept of this method was already known in Europe long before Whitney built his cotton gin or his musket factory. Court records from the various cotton gin lawsuits, however, provide ample evidence that Whitney was an early innovator who developed specific applications of this method.

Making Machines to Do the Work

Mass production of interchangeable parts requires that a product be designed with parts that are cut and shaped by machines. Each machine does one precise function over and over again to produce parts that are identical.

Whitney persuaded the U.S. government to contract with him to mass-produce ten thousand muskets for $13.40 each. The entire order of guns was to be delivered within two years. His reputation as the inventor of the cotton gin convinced the government to make such an agreement, even though he had never before built even one musket! It took eight years for Whitney to fulfill the contract.

Always the Inventor

In 1817, Eli Whitney ended what he called his "old bachelor" days and married Henrietta Edwards. He was no longer the shy farm boy, but a respected leader in banking, business, and education. They became the parents of three daughters and one son.

An ill Eli Whitney began studying human anatomy. His last papers include sketches of inventions for new medical devices he hoped would someday help others avoid the suffering from cancer he was experiencing. He died at his home in New Haven on January 8, 1825, doing what he had done throughout his life: inventing mechanical solutions to solve human problems.

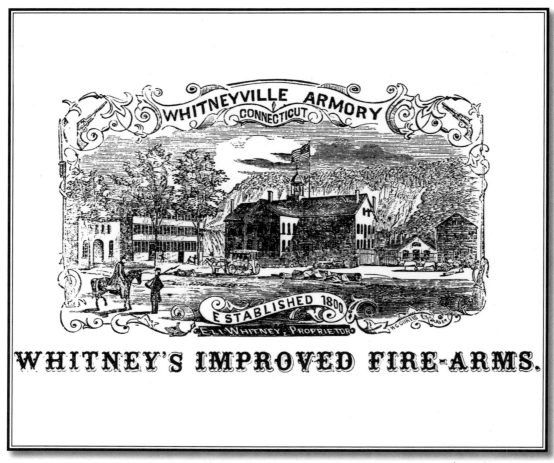

An advertisement for Whitney's firearms

CHAPTER FOUR

So Promising an Invention

"If I would pursue it and try to experiment, he would be out the whole expense. I should lose nothing but my time, and if I succeeded we would share the profits."—Eli Whitney in a letter to his father, 1793

Eli Whitney never claimed to be a mechanical genius. Most accounts of his life say he was a shy person who preferred to work alone to solve the problems he encountered while he pursued his invention ideas using the process of trial and error. This process was to try something and, if it failed, try something else until all the things that did not work had been eliminated.

Some of the first problems Whitney faced, according to Olmsted's biography, were "such rude materials and instruments as a Georgia plantation afforded." In other words, before Whitney could construct an entire cotton gin for ginning upland cotton, he first had to make some of the parts. To make some of the parts, he first had to make some of the materials from which to make the parts!

Olmsted says the thin pieces of wire Whitney eventually used to make the hooks to snag the lint from the seeds are an example of a material he had to make.

The Cotton Ginners Handbook

Eli Whitney did not have the benefit of *The Cotton Ginners Handbook* to help him invent the cotton gin. The U.S. Agricultural Research Service first published the 337-page handbook, written and edited by W. S. Anthony and William Mayfield in 1964. Each new edition contains updated technical information and is the most used tool in the cotton gin industry. The 2004 edition is available from the Superintendent of Documents and sells for $35.50. It is the only book of its kind in the world.

A Logical Starting Point

Whitney was not concerned that he knew so little about cotton. Nor was he concerned that other inventors had attempted to build a machine to gin short-staple cotton. Studying earlier machines, including the churka gin, provided a logical starting point for his experiments.

Natural curiosity and observation helped Whitney apply his knowledge. Southern plantations had to produce many of the products needed to sustain those who lived on them. Although Mulberry Grove was primarily a rice plantation, it is very likely that some cotton was grown to provide for the clothing and household needs of the plantation owner and slaves. Whitney might have observed a slave separating cotton from seed by hand, or using one of the churka-type gins to clean cotton that might have been grown there.

Two additional things made Whitney confident he could invent a cotton gin: his willingness to persist with his experiments and his personal motivation.

Tools of the Times

Tools in Eli Whitney's plantation shed included hammers, saws, chisels, wood-smoothing planes, knives, axes, hole punches, a lathe, an anvil, a bellows, and a fireplace that served as a forge. All of the tools were powered by hand.

Every mechanical calculation had to be done by hand using early American measurements. For example, one-third of an inch was referred to as "1 barleycorn."

Previous Successes

If Olmsted's version of Whitney's early life is accurate, Whitney remembered his boyhood success inventing the machine to make nails. He also remembered building a violin, manufacturing ladies' hatpins, and repairing the teaching instruments used by his instructors at Yale.

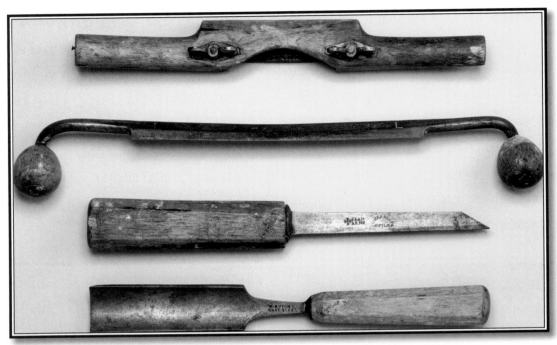

Whitney may have used tools similar to these as he worked on his inventions.

From these accomplishments, he had developed a simple method for inventing: First, he determined the results the invention needed to produce. Then he experimented to find a practical way for the invention to produce the desired results. He used this method to invent a model of a cotton gin in only ten days.

Willingness to Persist

Whitney persisted in experimenting to improve each separate part of the gin model so it would work better when combined with the other parts. For example, when the "teeth" did not work well, he made hook-shaped wire "teeth" to replace them on the cylinder, instead of trying to invent a completely new machine.

Personal Motivation

The desire to make a better cotton gin motivated Whitney to keep going when he encountered difficulties in the invention process. Another, equally important, personal desire also motivated Whitney to continue his experiments.

"It is said I will make a fortune from it," he wrote to his father. The possibility of making a fortune certainly appealed to Whitney, who desperately needed money to pay his debts. Whitney pursued his idea with ambition, but soon learned that perfecting a machine and profiting from it were two very different things.

Patent Pursuits

On June 20, 1793, Whitney wrote to Secretary of State Thomas Jefferson requesting a patent for his new cotton gin. He claimed in his letter that his invention was faster and more efficient "than any other machine heretofore known or used for that purpose."

Four months later, Whitney sent a drawing of his invention to Jefferson with his completed application for a patent. Jefferson was so impressed he told Whitney he wanted to purchase one of the machines for himself. He

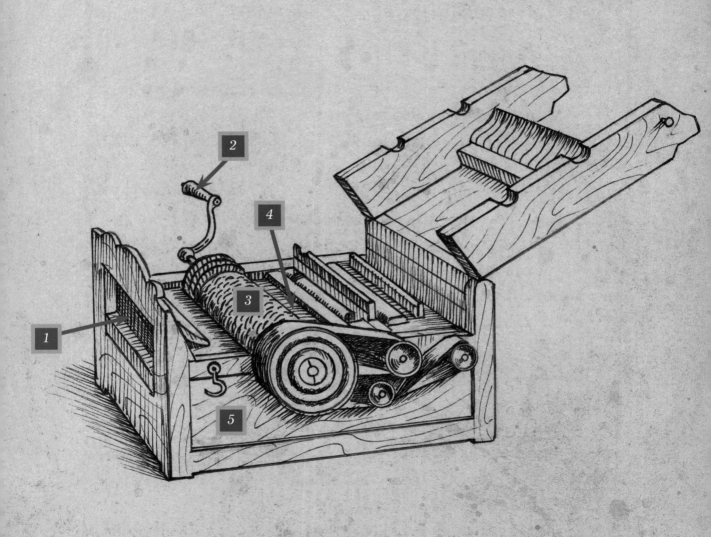

told Whitney he would have to submit an actual working model before a patent could be issued.

It took more months of experimentation, redesign, and manufacture for Whitney to build a working model. An outbreak of yellow fever and scarlet fever delayed Whitney from taking his working model to Philadelphia, which was

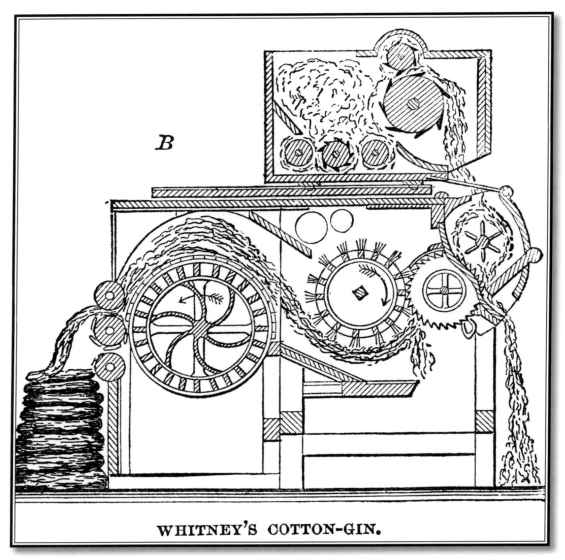

WHITNEY'S COTTON-GIN.

A woodcut diagram shows how an advanced model of Whitney's cotton gin worked.

then the capital of the United States. At last, on March 14, 1794, Whitney received a patent for a "spiked-tooth cotton gin." He returned to New Haven to set up a factory to

40

build gins, while Phineas Miller sold the services of their gins throughout the South.

The Patent Process

In order for the secretary of state to issue a patent for the cotton gin, Eli Whitney had to do four things:

1. Present working drawings or blueprints of the invention
2. Present a written description of the invention
3. Provide a working model of the invention
4. Pay an application fee

Patent requirements have changed through the years. Today, the U.S. Patent and Trademark Office is a part of the Commerce Department.

Patent Problems

President George Washington signed Whitney's patent in 1794. A South Carolina blacksmith named Hodgen Holmes invented a cotton gin similar to Whitney's, but his plan called for using iron circular saws with teeth on a turning cylinder.

Holmes claimed Whitney stole his idea for the cotton gin. Years of legal battles eventually proved Whitney did not. In 1796, the courts credited Holmes with the invention of the circular saw method as an improvement to the gin, but Whitney's claim of inventing the first machine for ginning short-staple cotton was recognized.

President George Washington signed Eli Whitney's cotton gin patent in 1794.

Stolen Secrets

Whitney agreed to demonstrate his cotton gin model to a few southern planters who were friends of Mrs. Greene before he received the approved patent. This proved to be a terrible mistake. Word spread like wildfire about his invention, how it worked, and how simple it would be to build.

Thieves broke into the shed at Mulberry Grove Plantation and stole the design for the model. Planters began building their own gins even before Whitney's New Haven factory was operating. They rushed to plant every acre with short-staple cotton to sell to the textile mills.

Planters in Georgia became furious when Whitney and Miller attempted to monopolize the cotton gin industry by demanding a fee of 1 pound (0.5 kg) of cotton for every 3 pounds (1.4 kg) ginned by their cotton gins. Rumors circulated that Whitney's gins damaged the cotton fibers by creating *neps,* small tangled knots, in the lint. Planters feared

When planters saw how simple it would be to build a cotton gin like Whitney's, many rushed to have their own gins built.

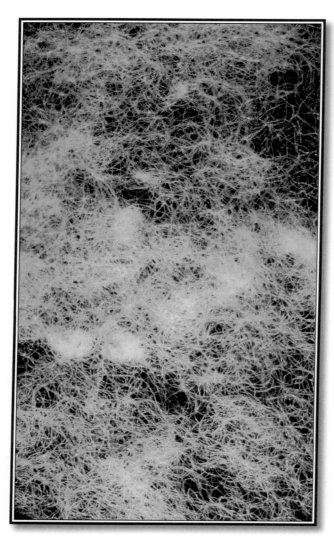

Neps are small tangled knots that ruin the cotton fibers.

they could not sell the fiber from Whitney's gins to the textile mills in England.

"I have battled the most depraved villains," Whitney angrily wrote to a friend after he heard about the rumor. Eventually, the partners collected a portion of the royalty money they were due. They spent all of it protecting their patent rights in legal battles and lawsuits.

In 1801, a judge for the circuit court of the District of Georgia declared Eli Whitney the inventor of the cotton gin. The judge stated in his decision, "The cotton gin opened views which set the whole country in active motion. The full extent of it cannot be seen." It soon became evident how true his words were.

CHAPTER FIVE

Avalanche of Change

"An invention can be so valuable as to be worthless to its inventor." —Eli Whitney, 1804

Cotton is grown on many farms in the southern United States.

The Cotton Belt began as a vast area of the southeastern United States where cotton was the main cash crop before the Civil War. Today, the Cotton Belt stretches from North Carolina to California. Between fifteen and twenty million **bales** of cotton are produced there each year, making the United States the second-largest cotton-producing country in the world.

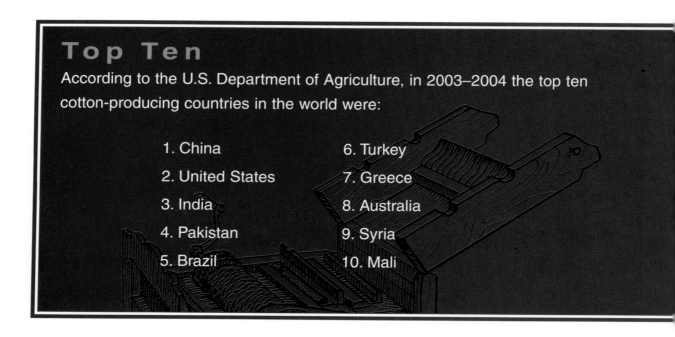

Top Ten

According to the U.S. Department of Agriculture, in 2003–2004 the top ten cotton-producing countries in the world were:

1. China
2. United States
3. India
4. Pakistan
5. Brazil
6. Turkey
7. Greece
8. Australia
9. Syria
10. Mali

Paving the Way

Southern planters were not prepared two hundred years ago for the transportation problem that accompanied the increase of ginned cotton. Wagons loaded with 400-pound (181-kg) bales had to travel from the plantation gin to canals, rivers, and seaports for shipment to textile mills. The wagons routinely sank into the roads that were hardly more than dirt trails. Slaves had to lay wooden planks to "pave" the wagon roads.

These plank-paved roads established the routes that are now part of the modern highway system of the South. Better roads are just one example of how people using Whitney's cotton gin started an avalanche of change in

Wagons loaded with bales of cotton traveled over dirt roads to get to rivers or ports where the cotton could be shipped to textile mills.

the South. This avalanche also altered the course of the entire nation.

The Road to Economic Prosperity

By 1801, cotton produced in Georgia and South Carolina had soared from 2 million to 37 million pounds (907,185 kg to 16,783,000 kg)! Production doubled in the United States each decade thereafter as horse-driven and water-powered gins began whirring in other southern states. In 1850, almost 60 percent of the United States' exports came from the cotton gins of the South.

Planters used their profits to purchase more land to grow more cotton. More cotton resulted in cheaper prices, and cheaper prices made cotton the most desired fabric in the textile industry. David Christy, author of *Cotton Is King*, later restated what many southerners had been saying for a long time: "The cotton gin made the cotton plant the sole possessor of the South. It was, in fact, the soul of the South."

Don't Throw Away the Seeds!

Cottonseeds removed by Whitney's gin were either used for replanting or discarded with the other gin trash because no one knew how valuable they were. Whitney's partner, Phineas Miller, is credited with pioneering the use of the seeds for fertilizer, *fodder,* and oil. It wasn't until a little more than a hundred years ago, however, that the many uses for cottonseed began to be discovered.

Manual-powered presses in the late 1800s recovered about one-half of the oil contained in the seed. Today's cottonseed mills can remove all but 1 to 2 percent of it. From 790 pounds (358 kg) of cottonseed, 140 pounds (64 kg) of cottonseed oil can be extracted from the seed kernels that have been separated from the seed hulls.

The seed kernels are pressed into thin flakes, cooked, and squeezed in screw press mills—or they are cooked, sliced to about the thickness of a sheet of paper, and exposed to steam at high pressure in solvent extraction mills. The de-oiled meat is dried and ground to produce high-protein livestock feed called cottonseed meal.

Cottonseed oil is used to make cosmetics, rubber, soap, insecticides, and other products. With more processing, cottonseed oil becomes suitable for use in making products such as vegetable oil, margarine, and mayonnaise.

The hull of the cottonseed surrounding the kernels is also used as feed for livestock as well as mulch for soil, and is used to manufacture plastics, synthetic rubber, and explosives.

The road to economic prosperity in the South had plenty of rough spots:

- Competition among wealthy southern planters increased the price of land so much that it hindered the growth of industry and cities.
- The price paid for cotton by textile mills rose and fell frequently. It was said that a planter could "get out of bed poor and go to bed rich," or vice versa!
- Drought and destruction from infestations of insects such as the boll weevil constantly threatened to ruin those who planted all of their cropland in cotton. Boll weevils, such as those that invaded the South in the late nineteenth century, could destroy a crop in one day.

Many southern planters were convinced they could overcome any economic adversity as long as they had cheap labor. Just as northern industrialists relied on low-paid workers, including children, to keep factories and mills operating, planters relied on slave labor to keep the South's agricultural economy moving.

From Bags to Bales

Ginned cotton was originally packed into long, round bags. Each bag filled with cotton weighed 150 to 250 pounds (68 kg to 113 kg) and could be carried by two people. By 1800, large presses were used to squeeze cotton into 400-pound (181-kg) square bales. Mules or oxen harnessed to a lever walked in a circle turning a wooden screw press that packed the cotton into square molds. The bales turned out of the molds were weighed, covered with cloth, tied with ropes or metal bands, and stacked several layers high onto wagons for transport.

Screw presses were used extensively for almost one hundred years. Today, there are four types of gin presses. Each type is named according to the bale it produces—flat bale, modified flat bale, gin standard density bale, and gin universal density bale. These presses produce different sizes of bales. In most cotton gins today, cotton is packaged in a double-box press. The lint is first compacted in one press box by a piece of machinery called a tramper. The press box is rotated, and the lint is pressed into gin universal density bales, bales that are pressed to weigh 28 pounds (13 kg) per square foot each. More than 90 percent of the bales produced at gins in the United States are gin universal density bales.

The Road to Social Tragedy

Although Whitney's cotton gin had many positive effects on the economy of the South, it had disastrous effects on the institution of slavery. Instead of reducing the need for slaves as he had hoped, the cotton gin created the need for more and more workers to plant, harvest, bale, and transport cotton grown on the plantations, which were spreading westward.

The slave trade flourished. From 1790 until Congress banned the importation of slaves in 1808, more than eighty thousand slaves were brought to the United States. By 1860, there were fifteen slave states instead of six. One out of every three people living in the South was a slave.

The Road to Political Catastrophe

"You dare not make war on cotton! Cotton is king." These fiery words, spoken by South Carolina senator James Henry Hammond in 1858, were directed at New York senator William H. Seward, a determined abolitionist. Seward had warned Hammond that war might be necessary in order to stop slavery in the southern states.

Like most southerners, Hammond believed cotton was a more powerful weapon than any sword the North could wield to abolish slavery. The political battles among the cotton-producing states of the South and the antislavery states of the North climaxed in 1861 in the political catastrophe known as the American Civil War.

The Confederate States of America, consisting of eleven Southern states that seceded from the United States, relied on sales of cotton to foreign countries for the money it needed to buy supplies. This reliance on cotton

A convoy of cotton is set on fire in South Carolina during the American Civil War.

contributed heavily to the defeat of the Confederacy. Union naval blockades successfully prevented Confederate cotton shipments from reaching England and France. By 1864, the flow of money into the Confederate treasury from foreign nations had slowed to a trickle.

Weapon of Weakness

Southern soldiers fighting on Civil War battlefields could not take time out to plant or harvest a cotton crop. Most of the gins had been destroyed in the cross fire, and there was no material available to construct new ones. This meant that loans the Confederate government had secured could not be paid back in cotton as promised.

Some Southerners burned their own cotton to keep it from falling into Union hands. Others secretly traded their crops to Union suppliers for food and weapons. Rather than a powerful weapon, cotton turned out to be a weakness the South could not overcome.

At the end of the Civil War in 1865, the South had no cotton, no money, and no power. Cotton was no longer king. The Union victory brought an end to the plantation system and to slavery in the United States. It also temporarily muffled the whir of the cotton gins because few southern plantation owners had the financial resources or the manpower to plant and harvest cotton immediately after the war.

The Road to Recovery

By the time the smoke had lifted from the battlefields, northern textile mills were in desperate need of cotton to manufacture wagon covers, tents, and rugged clothing

Eli Whitney's cotton gin increased rather than decreased the problem of slavery because it created the demand for more cotton to be planted and harvested.

demanded by displaced southerners and new immigrants moving west. Many northerners had suffered the loss of family and friends, and they joined the westward movement to seek new lives.

Southern farmers, including a small number of freed slaves who now had land of their own, began producing cotton crops. They also began building gins with improvements, such as mechanical feeders (introduced in the 1840s) to feed cotton into the gin saws, and condensers (introduced in the 1850s) placed at the rear of the gins to catch the lint and form it into *batts* to make it easier to bale. These mechanized improvements greatly speeded the ginning process while reducing the need for human labor.

Levis Not Levi's

Bavarian immigrant Levi Strauss popularized blue jeans, but he did not invent them, as is commonly believed. That distinction goes to a man named Jacob Davis.

Strauss was a well-known clothing merchant in San Francisco when Davis, who lived in Reno, Nevada, contacted him with an idea for using copper rivets to reinforce pocket corners and other heavily stressed parts of pants. Strauss readily agreed to make the pants Davis designed. Strauss first used heavy *canvas* cloth, then used a twilled cotton cloth from France called serge de Nimes, which became known as *denim.*

In 1873, the two men filed a joint patent for "riveted waist overalls." It wasn't until 1960 that the company began referring to its product as jeans instead of overalls in advertisements. The word jeans comes from the name Genoa, the Italian port famous for its cotton.

The Road to Mexia

Eli Whitney's gin not only produced ginned cotton, but it also produced competition among inventors who wanted to profit from the demand for more cotton. Hodgen Holmes's 1796 patented invention was a gin that used metal saws positioned on a rotating shaft. His gin allowed the cleaned seeds to fall out the bottom, making it possible for cotton to be continually fed into the gin to separate the green seeds from the lint, instead of ginning a batch at a time.

Gins were built in blacksmith shops and small manufacturing shops by highly skilled mechanics known as **ginwrights.** By 1840, gins were in operation throughout the cotton-growing lands of the southern United States. A few gins were operating with as many as forty saws. That same year, Fones McCarthy invented a more efficient roller gin that consisted of a leather ginning roller, a stationary knife held tightly against the roller, and another knife that pulled the seed from the lint as the lint was held by the roller and stationary knife.

Ginning technology took a giant step forward in 1883 when Robert S. Munger introduced the system ginning process in Mexia, Texas. System ginning rapidly dried, cleaned, and ginned the seed cotton, and baled the lint cotton in one continuous process. Steam engines powered the ginning plant. These were replaced with diesel engines in 1910. Electric motors took the place of the diesel engines and are

Robert S. Munger was born in 1854 in Texas. He revolutionized cotton ginning by introducing a combined process that became known as system ginning.

still the power source used in today's modern cotton gin. Munger's gin system combined all the parts of the process into one continuous operation—from the air suction "telescope" pipe used to draw the cotton bolls from the wagon, to the first indoor bale press.

With this all-in-one system, farmers working smaller parcels of land did not have to build individual gins. They formed gin cooperatives, which allowed them to share in the profits, as well as the costs, of building one gin used by many. There are approximately 1,400 cotton gins in the United States today, including gins built by groups of individuals who formed partnerships to own, operate, and share in the profits.

Munger's system revolutionized cotton farming. By 1900, an avalanche of forty thousand whirring gins announced to the world that cotton was king again in the Cotton Belt.

CHAPTER SIX

Ginning Fiber for the Future

"What is so hard about cotton? It is hard to separate the lint from the seeds. It is hard to control insects, weeds and diseases. It is hard to grow without adequate water. It is hard to assemble the harvested product into a form easy to transport to market. It is hard to predict the market price. The hardest thing about cotton, however, is trying to imagine life without it."
—Ron Smith, *Southwest Farm Press*, May 2004

The only function of both the churka roller gin and Eli Whitney's spiked-tooth gin was to remove cottonseed from the fiber. The basic purpose of each of these gin designs has not changed. Saw-teeth gins are still used for cleaning short- to medium-staple cotton. Modern roller gins are used for ginning long-staple cotton.

In the late 1780s, Joseph Eve invented and began manufacturing an improved roller gin to separate black seeds from long-fibered Sea Island cotton. Eve was living in the Bahamas islands about the time Eli Whitney was perfecting his gin to separate green seeds from short-fibered cotton. Eve's improvements to the roller gin included using horses, wind, and water to power it. He brought his powered roller gin to the United States when Sea Island cotton was introduced as a commercial crop in Georgia and South Carolina in 1790.

During the first half of the twentieth century, severe drought, economic depression, and boll weevil infestations almost ended cotton production in the United States. What emerged from that period were the three most critical needs of the ginning industry, called the Three Rs—Research, Reduce, and Revitalize. These three needs continue to shape the future of the cotton gin.

Pima Cotton

Extra-long staple cotton was developed in 1825 when long-staple Sea Island cotton was crossed with another variety of cotton named Jumel in Egypt. This new extra-long staple variety was developed further before the plants were brought to the southwestern United States about 1900.

The first commercial extra-long staple crop in the United States was produced in 1912. This variety was named in honor of the Pima Indians, who helped produce the first crop at the U.S. Department of Agriculture experimental farm in Arizona.

Today, less than 5 percent of the cotton produced in the United States is the Pima variety. It is ginned on modern roller gins, and the thread is woven into a very popular silky cotton fabric used to make clothing and household goods.

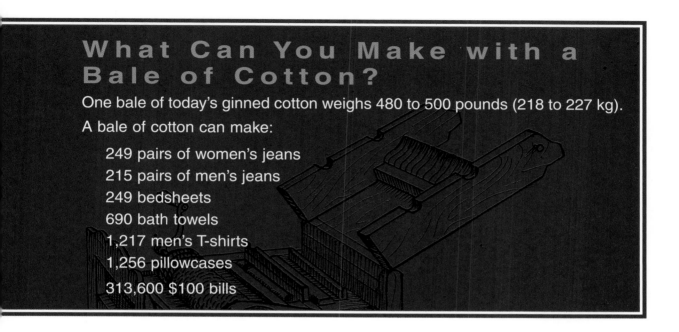

What Can You Make with a Bale of Cotton?

One bale of today's ginned cotton weighs 480 to 500 pounds (218 to 227 kg).
A bale of cotton can make:

- 249 pairs of women's jeans
- 215 pairs of men's jeans
- 249 bedsheets
- 690 bath towels
- 1,217 men's T-shirts
- 1,256 pillowcases
- 313,600 $100 bills

Research

The stage was set for quantum leaps in gin advancements when the U.S. Cotton Ginning Research Laboratory was established in 1928 in Stoneville, Mississippi. Many of the developments in modern ginning originated there, along with developments at similar research facilities established later, such as the Southwestern Cotton Ginning Research Laboratory at Mesilla Park, New Mexico (which includes a complete saw and roller-ginning laboratory) and the Southern Regional Research Center in New Orleans, Louisiana. Federal ginning laboratories work with the U.S. Agriculture Research Service to find ways to improve gins and ginning to make the finished fiber more valuable.

Ginned cotton is spun into threads that are woven into fabric used in many different products.

The most exciting new technology shaping the present and future of the cotton gin is Computerized Gin Process Control (CGPC), introduced in 1997. CGPC technology is used to automatically measure the cotton's quality (the size and strength of each individual cotton fiber) at various stages of ginning. CGPC evaluates lint moisture (the amount of moisture in the fibers), **color** (the degree of whiteness based upon international standards), and trash content (the leaf content of ginned cotton). From there, a "recipe" is created, prescribing the best combination of ginning processes, and then the cotton is ginned to the exact measurements called for in the recipe.

"The world is sending us a message. Our gins must produce quality fiber or our cotton will not be competitive in the global marketplace," says researcher Mike Watson. "We must produce the fiber of the future."

How Cotton Is Ginned and Graded Today

1. After mechanical harvesting, cotton is either stored in *modules,* which look like giant loaves of bread, or is transported in trailers.
2. Module feeders break the modules apart and feed the seed cotton into the gin, or powerful pipes suck the loose cotton into the gin from the trailer.
3. Once inside the cotton gin, the seed cotton moves through dryers and cleaning machines that remove the trash, such as hulls, dirt, stems, and leaves.
4. The cotton goes to the gin stand where circular saws with small, sharp teeth pluck the fiber from the seed.
5. Ginned fiber, now called lint, is pressed together and made into dense bales weighing about 500 pounds (227 kg).
6. The value and *grade* of the bale is determined by a cotton sample taken from each bale and classed according to staple, thickness, color, and cleanness. At one time, a man with a sharp knife known as a cotton sampler cut each bale of cotton ginned. Now samples are cut mechanically.

Reduce

Among today's greatest challenges for ginners is to increase uniformity in cotton fiber delivered to textile mills. Ginners must also reduce cotton dust and noise to protect

A worker wears a mask to avoid breathing in dust from cotton as it is sorted for spinning.

the health of workers and the environment. Attempts to reduce "sticky cotton" (sometimes referred to as honeydew) are also a priority. A closer look reveals why reducing these problems is vital to the future of ginning.

Neps are small fiber entanglements that create knots. They are caused by manipulation of the cotton fibers during the ginning process. Textile mills today demand ginned cotton with few flaws in the fiber and staple lengths that

A farmer and a technician from the U.S. Department of Agriculture inspect cotton plants for boll weevils.

cannot be even 1/100 of an inch too short or too long. This is necessary for complex machinery to spin the fiber into yarn that is transformed into quality fabric by knitting or weaving.

Byssinosis is an occupational disease associated with inhaling airborne cotton dust. Reducing the risk of respiratory disease is an ongoing effort in all areas of the cotton industry, as is lowering noise levels in cotton gins. Environmental challenges have produced some of the more obvious changes in cotton ginning. For example, cotton **burs** are no longer burned, which was once the method of disposal.

Sticky cotton is caused primarily by insects known as whiteflies and aphids. A stickiness tester to detect insect sugar on cotton has been developed at the U.S. Cotton Ginning Laboratory, but eliminating the insects that cause the stickiness continues to be a challenge as difficult as the hundred-year battle to eradicate the boll weevil.

Boll Weevils and Spiderwort

Boll weevils arrived in the United States from Mexico in 1892 and have cost the U.S. cotton industry an estimated $14 billion in yield losses and costs to control the beetle. A cooperative boll weevil eradication program has been successful in eliminating weevils from Virginia, the Carolinas, Georgia, Florida, southern Alabama, California, Arizona, and parts of Texas.

Now a little-known weed is spreading fast and may become even more of a threat than the boll weevil. Tropical spiderwort competes with crops for water and nutrients, and smothers the crops at the same time. Spiderwort spread as cotton acreage in Georgia increased (because of the success of the boll weevil eradication program) from 260,000 acres (105,218 hectares) in 1989 to nearly 1.5 million acres (607,000 hectares) in 1995. It has continued to spread to other states.

In a modern cotton gin, several gin stands can be operated at the same time using the Computer Gin Process Control system.

Revitalize

Rapid expansion of automated and computerized process control systems will revitalize the ginning industry. Less-aggressive and less-damaging machines are already being developed and affordably integrated into existing gin systems. For example, individual cotton processing machines can modify fiber quality characteristics every few seconds during the ginning process without any interruption in the production flow.

New gins capable of producing up to sixty bales of high-quality cotton per hour are being built in some areas of the United States where cotton production had almost disappeared. In 1991, there were only about 4,000 acres (1,619 hectares) of cotton in Martin County, North Carolina. Today, there are more than 48,000 acres (19,425 hectares) of cotton there, with a modern gin processing between forty thousand and sixty thousand bales of cotton each year.

The cotton industry has faced, and met, incredible challenges since Eli Whitney arrived at Mulberry Grove Plantation. More than two hundred years later, the cotton gin of the future is whirring on the horizon!

The Cotton Gin: A Timeline

Joseph Eve invents an improved roller gin for long-staple cotton.
p. 59

Hodgen Holmes receives a patent for a circular-saw improvement to the gin.
p. 42

Cotton fibers woven into cloth.
p. 11

Christopher Columbus finds cotton plants growing in the Bahamas islands. *p. 17*

Whitney submits his first request for a patent.
p. 38

Circuit court of the District of Georgia declares Eli Whitney the inventor of the cotton gin.
p. 44

| c. 4000 B.C. | | 1492 | | c. 1790 | | 1793 | | 1796 | | 1801 |
| c. 1000 B.C. | | | 1730 | | 1793 | | 1794 | | 1800 | |

Invention of the churka gin.
p. 13

Eli Whitney begins experiments on his cotton gin for short-staple cotton at Mulberry Grove Plantation in partnership with Phineas Miller.
p. 29

Large presses begin producing square bales.
p. 50

Industrial Revolution begins in England.
p. 19

Patent for a "spiked-tooth cotton gin" issued to Whitney.
p. 41

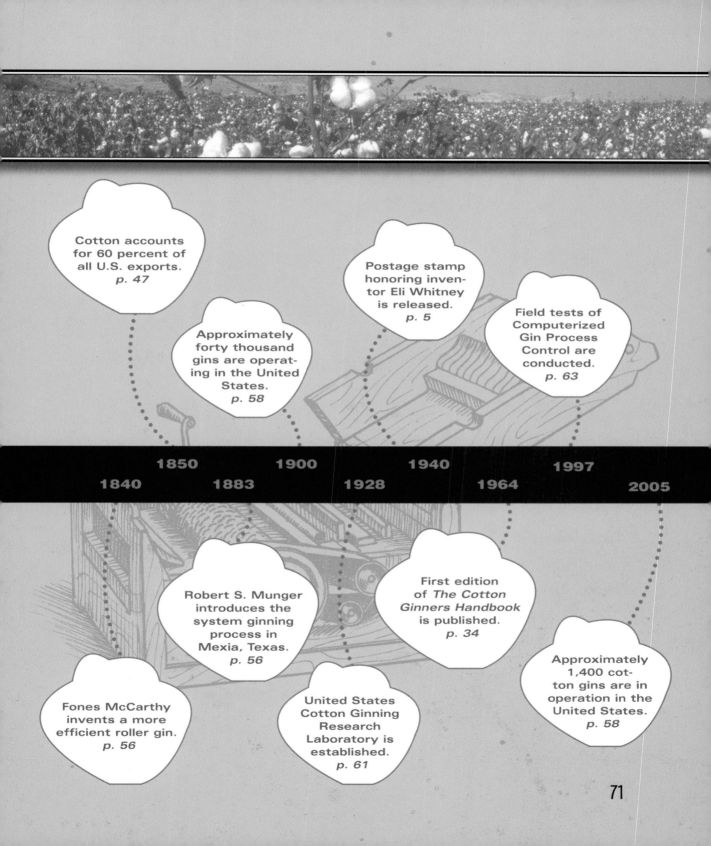

Cotton accounts for 60 percent of all U.S. exports.
p. 47

Approximately forty thousand gins are operating in the United States.
p. 58

Postage stamp honoring inventor Eli Whitney is released.
p. 5

Field tests of Computerized Gin Process Control are conducted.
p. 63

1840   1850   1883   1900   1928   1940   1964   1997   2005

Fones McCarthy invents a more efficient roller gin.
p. 56

Robert S. Munger introduces the system ginning process in Mexia, Texas.
p. 56

United States Cotton Ginning Research Laboratory is established.
p. 61

First edition of *The Cotton Ginners Handbook* is published.
p. 34

Approximately 1,400 cotton gins are in operation in the United States.
p. 58

Glossary

agronomist: scientist who studies crops

bale: cotton lint compressed into approximately 500-pound squares

batts: sheets or rolls of ginned cotton

boll: pod on the cotton plant where seeds and lint grow

boll weevil: a beetle that destroys cotton bolls

burs: dried hulls of the cotton bolls

canvas: heavy, closely woven cotton cloth

color: one of thirty shades of white used as an international standard to grade cotton

denim: strong cotton cloth that originated in France

fiber: cotton lint

fodder: food for cattle and other farm animals

forge: a furnace for refining or melting metal

gin: short for "cotton engine"; a machine used to separate cottonseeds from fibers

ginwright: a person who builds and maintains a mechanical cotton gin

grade: the quality of cotton based on the color of the fiber, trash content, appearance, feel, and staple length

interchangeable parts: identical pieces that can substitute one for another

loom: machine for weaving cloth

module: approximately 10,000 pounds (4,536 kg) of raw cotton pressed together for transport from the field to a gin

monopoly: the complete control of something, especially a service or the supply of a product

neps: small knots of tangled cotton fiber

patent: government protection to an inventor giving exclusive rights to an invention

Permanent Bale Identification: a system of assigning an identification code to every bale of cotton ginned

raw cotton: harvested cotton prior to ginning

spinning wheel: a machine that converts fiber into yarn or thread

staple: length and fineness of cotton fiber after seeds and trash have been removed

textile: woven fabric of natural or artificial fiber

trash: leaf content of ginned cotton

To Find Out More

Books

Britton, Karen G. *Bale o' Cotton: The Mechanical Art of Cotton Ginning.* College Station, Tex.: A&M University Press, 1992.

Masters, Nancy Robinson. *The Fabulous Flying Flag Farm.* Abilene, Tex.: MasAir Publications, 1998.

Web Sites

National Cotton Council of America
http://www.cotton.org
Facts and other educational information about the cotton industry

Burton Cotton Gin and Museum
http://www.cottonginmuseum.org
Online museum that interprets life in a historic Texas cotton town

Eli Whitney

http://www.eliwhitney.org

More information about inventor Eli Whitney

Organizations

National Cotton Ginners Association

1918 North Parkway

Memphis, TN 38112-5018

For information on the cotton ginning industry

National Cottonseed Products Association

104 Timber Creek Drive, Suite 200

Cordova, TN 38018

http://www.cottonseed.com

To learn more about the many uses of cottonseed

Museums

South Carolina Cotton Museum

121 West Cedar Lane

Bishopville, SC 29010

http://www.sccotton.org

Visit to learn more about the history of cotton

The Louisiana Cotton Museum

7162 Highway 65 North

Lake Providence, LA 71254

To learn about the history or cotton and its impact on the economy of Louisiana and the United States

Index

About the Author

Nancy Robinson Masters grew up on a cotton farm in west Texas. She began her career as a writer when she was in elementary school.

Her father worked as a cotton sampler at gins. On Saturdays during the cotton harvest season, she went with with him to the gin. As they walked up and down the rows of cotton bales, he told her stories and she wrote them down in her fourth-grade spiral notebook.

Nancy has shared her dad's cotton gin stories in books, magazines, and newspapers, and in visiting author programs for students. In addition to her writing career, she is a licensed pilot. She lives on a farm near Abilene, Texas, with her husband, aviator Bill Masters. Nancy is also the author of *The Airplane*, another book in the Inventions That Shaped the World series.